AN
ADVENT CAR
COUNTDOW

Stories behind the Most Beloved Mus

AN
ADVENT CAROLS COUNTDOWN

Stories behind the Most Beloved Music of Christmas

MICHAEL D. YOUNG

SHADOW
MOUNTAIN
PUBLISHING

To Jenny, Jarem, Bryson, and Maggie

Library of Congress Cataloging-in-Publication Data

Names: Young, Michael D., 1984– author.

Title: An Advent carols countdown : stories behind the most beloved music of Christmas / Michael D. Young.

Description: [Salt Lake City] : Shadow Mountain Publishing, [2022] | Includes the text of 24 Christmas carols with historical commentary arranged as an Advent calendar. | Includes bibliographical references. | Summary: "Author Michael D. Young relates the stories behind twenty-four of the most beloved carols of Christmas in a format that lends itself to reading one per day in a countdown to Christmas Day"—Provided by publisher.

Identifiers: LCCN 2022005832 | ISBN 9781639930470 (hardback)

Subjects: LCSH: Christmas music—History and criticism. | Carols—History and criticism. | Advent calendars. | LCGFT: Carol texts. | Hymn texts.

Classification: LCC ML2880 .Y65 2022 | DDC 781.723—dc23

LC record available at https://lccn.loc.gov/2022005832

Printed in the United States of America

1 2 3 4 5 LBC 26 25 24 23 22

Contents

Acknowledgments

I have had so many amazing music teachers and directors over the years who have fostered my love for music, especially Christmas carols. In particular, I'd like to thank my high school choir directors, Elizabeth Bassler and David Barthelmess for directing such amazing madrigal groups that deepened my appreciation for a variety of carols. I would also like to acknowledge the directors of the Tabernacle Choir at Temple Square, Mack Wilberg and Ryan Murphy, who also introduced me to carols from all over the world through their wonderful arrangements. Every Christmas concert I sang under their direction introduced me to new carols to love and research. Finally, I'd like to thank my parents, who made music an indispensable part of every Christmas celebration.

Introduction

It's hard to imagine Christmas without music. Christmas carols are an integral part of the Christmas celebration in numerous cultures throughout the world and have been written for hundreds of years. Many of the carols we sing year in and year out are hundreds of years old but remain favorites today. And no matter where carols are from, they almost always focus us on the true reason for the season: our Savior, Jesus Christ. Carols act as a connecting thread of faith between us, our ancestors, and those all over the world who also celebrate the birth of Christ.

Indeed, one of the wonderful things about Christmas carols is that they come from so many different places. Some were written by monks and priests, as you might expect, but others were written by people who were not religious at all. Sometimes those who wrote the lyrics and those who wrote the music lived hundreds of years apart, and sometimes carols were created by adapting existing songs.

An Advent Carols Countdown will help you learn about the origin of carols both familiar and (to some) new. Each day leading up to Christmas, read about a different Christmas carol, and learn some of the history and background of the carol as well as a few details about the people who brought the carol to life.

1

The Holly and the Ivy

Lyrics

The holly and the ivy
when they are both full grown,
of all the trees that are in the wood
the holly bears the crown.

The rising of the sun
and the running of the deer;
the playing of the merry organ,
sweet singing in the choir.

The holly bears a blossom,
white as the lily flower,
and Mary bore sweet Jesus Christ,
to be our sweet Saviour.

The rising of the sun
and the running of the deer;
the playing of the merry organ,
sweet singing in the choir.

The holly bears a berry,
as red as any blood,
and Mary bore sweet Jesus Christ
to do poor sinners good.

The rising of the sun
and the running of the deer;
the playing of the merry organ,
sweet singing in the choir.

The holly bears a prickle,
as sharp as any thorn,
and Mary bore sweet Jesus Christ
on Christmas Day in the morn.

The rising of the sun
and the running of the deer;
the playing of the merry organ,
sweet singing in the choir.

The holly bears a bark,
as bitter as any gall,
and Mary bore sweet Jesus Christ
for to redeem us all.

The rising of the sun
and the running of the deer;
the playing of the merry organ,
sweet singing in the choir.

Scan this QR code to watch a musical performance of "The Holly and the Ivy"

About the Carol

This carol, which may date back to the seventeenth century, uses two evergreen plants to beautifully describe the symbolism behind the life of Jesus Christ. Holly and ivy plants were used in winter celebrations long before Christmas became a holiday. Their vibrant, green boughs—even amidst a cold, dark winter—were a sign of life. Some ancient peoples even believed the plants held magical qualities that could ward off evil. The Romans used holly and ivy in pagan celebrations, such as the midwinter festival of Saturnalia, which honored Saturnus, the god of agriculture.

Over time, it appears that Christians borrowed from these celebrations, adapting the symbols for their own use. In Victorian England, the use of holly and ivy to decorate for the Christmas season became so popular that a merchant in 1851 is said to have ordered a quarter-million bushels of holly to decorate that year.

In the carol, holly and ivy are used to describe the Christian symbolism attributed to the evergreen plants.

The white holly flower represents Mary's and Jesus's purity. The red holly berry symbolizes Christ's redeeming blood. The sharp prickle of the holly leaf is a reminder that the King of kings was forced to wear a crown of thorns on His head. And, of course, the evergreen nature of the plants points to the renewal of life through Christ.

Though the song is titled "The Holly and the Ivy," ivy is mentioned only in the song's first stanza. This may be a holdover from an earlier song called "The Contest of the Holly and the Ivy," which described a battle of the sexes, where holly represented the masculine sex and ivy represented the feminine.

Both the lyrics and the tune of the carol itself are anonymous. It was first officially published in 1911 by the great English folklorist Cecil Sharp. Sharp traveled all over Britain, collecting folk songs in villages small and large, recording melodies and poems that had been passed down for generations.

In 1909, Sharp reportedly talked to a Mary Clayton of Chipping Campden (located in Gloucestershire, England), who sang him a tune about holly and ivy. She said she'd learned the song as a child.

The tune she shared—which may be more than one thousand years old—is the one we recognize today as "The Holly and the Ivy." The words, however, only somewhat resembled what we are familiar with today. Her lyrics didn't make sense to Sharp, and so he asked about the song around town. He found a number of others who also knew the tune—with varying lyrics—and was able to record the melody and words in his notebook. This helped him arrange a complete version that includes the refrain as we know it now.

2

O Little Town of Bethlehem

Lyrics

O little town of Bethlehem,
how still we see thee lie;
above thy deep and dreamless sleep
the silent stars go by;

Yet in thy dark streets shineth
the everlasting light;
the hopes and fears of all the years
are met in thee tonight.

For Christ is born of Mary,
and gathered all above,
while mortals sleep, the angels keep
their watch of wondering love.

O morning stars together,
proclaim the holy birth,

and praises sing to God the King,
and peace to all on earth!

How silently, how silently,
the wondrous gift is given;
so God imparts to human hearts
the blessings of his heaven.

No ear may hear his coming,
but in this world of sin,
where meek souls will receive him,
still the dear Christ enters in.

O holy Child of Bethlehem,
descend to us, we pray;
cast out our sin, and enter in,
be born in us today.

We hear the Christmas angels
the great glad tidings tell;
O come to us, abide with us,
our Lord Emmanuel!

 Scan this QR code to watch a musical performance of "O Little Town of Bethlehem"

About the Carol

The lyrics to this carol were penned by the great American preacher and author Phillips Brooks and were originally intended for the Sunday School children in his Philadelphia parish. Brooks wrote the verses in 1868, inspired by a memorable experience in Bethlehem, where he had traveled in December 1865 to find peace after the horrors of the Civil War and the assassination of Abraham Lincoln.

Brooks was a giant of a man—standing at six feet four inches—with a giant heart. He never married or had children of his own, but he loved being around children. In his office, he kept toys for children to play with when they visited him, and he was often seen down on the floor with children, joining in their games. One biographer wrote of Brooks that "there were children in many households where he visited, who rejoiced in his coming and claimed him as a friend."

During Brooks's 1865 sabbatical to the Holy Land, he rode on horseback from Jerusalem to Bethlehem on Christmas Eve. That and the experience immediately following it stuck with him for years before he could adequately describe his feelings about the night in verse. In his journal he wrote: "Before dark, we rode out of town to the field where they say the shepherds saw the star. It is a fenced piece of ground with a cave in it, in which, strangely enough, they put the shepherds. . . . Somewhere in those fields we rode through, the shepherds must have been. As we passed, the shepherds were still keeping watch over their flocks or leading them home to fold."

After the ride, he took part in a Christmas Eve service at the Church of the Nativity in Bethlehem. The service lasted well into the night. Of it, Brooks wrote: "I remember . . . on Christmas Eve, when I was standing in the old church at Bethlehem, close to the spot where Jesus was born, when the whole church was ringing hour after hour with the splendid hymns of praise to God, how again and again it seemed as if I could hear voices that I knew well, telling each other of the 'Wonderful Night' of the Saviour's birth."

Nearly three years later, as Brooks contemplated the upcoming Christmas services at his own church—the Church of the Holy Trinity in Philadelphia—he finally penned the lyrics we now know as "O Little Town of Bethlehem." He knew then that he wanted the words to be set to music, so he turned to his friend and the church's organist, Lewis Redner, to create a melody the children could sing to. Redner tried many different tunes but couldn't settle on anything that felt right. The night before the children's choir was set to rehearse the song for the first time, Redner had all but given up and gone to bed. During the night, he thought he heard music in his mind. He awoke and wrote down the tune. Redner believed it was a gift from heaven that the tune fit perfectly with the carol's lyrics. He filled in the harmony early Sunday morning, and the song was finished in time for rehearsal.

Redner's tune—named "St. Louis"—is still used today by both children and adults across the United States. Another tune—called "Forest Green" and used by the English composer Ralph Vaughn Williams in his arrangement of the carol—is more popular on the other side of the Atlantic and has become the traditional tune in England.

When sung, the hymn typically includes only three or four verses. Brooks's original poem, however, included these lyrics in a final verse:

>Where children pure and happy
>pray to the blessed Child,
>where misery cries out to thee,
>Son of the undefiled;
>
>Where charity stands watching
>and faith holds wide the door,
>the dark night wakes, the glory breaks,
>and Christmas comes once more.

3

Angels We Have Heard on High

Lyrics

Angels we have heard on high
sweetly singing o'er the plains,
and the mountains in reply
echoing their joyous strains.

Gloria, in excelsis Deo!
Gloria, in excelsis Deo!

Shepherds, why this jubilee?
Why your joyous strains prolong?
What the gladsome tidings be
which inspire your heavenly song?

Gloria, in excelsis Deo!
Gloria, in excelsis Deo!

Come to Bethlehem and see
Christ whose birth the angels sing;

come, adore on bended knee,
Christ the Lord, the newborn King.

Gloria, in excelsis Deo!
Gloria, in excelsis Deo!

See him in a manger laid,
whom the choirs of angels praise;
Mary, Joseph, lend your aid,
while our hearts in love we raise.

Gloria, in excelsis Deo!
Gloria, in excelsis Deo!

Scan this QR code to hear a musical performance of "Angels We Have Heard on High"

About the Carol

The origins of this beloved French carol are somewhat murky. The lyrics and tune were first published as *"Les Anges dans nos campagnes"* in 1855 in the French songbook *Nouveau recueil de cantiques*. But because of the song's Latin refrain—*gloria in excelsis Deo* (glory to God in the highest)—and references claiming the song had been in use for some time before its publication, some scholars push back its origins hundreds of years earlier.

The song's Latin refrain is the same phrase a choir of

heavenly hosts proclaimed to the shepherds on the night of the Savior's birth, as recorded in Luke 2:14. Using the phrase in worship dates back to A.D. 129, when Pope Telesphorus is said to have requested that it be sung as part of the Christmas Eve Mass. Thereafter, the phrase became known as the "Angel's Hymn" and has been adapted into numerous carols, including this one.

"Angels We Have Heard on High" is considered a "macaronic" hymn because the lyrics switch back and forth between Latin and another language. In French, the original eight stanzas also switch back and forth in perspective, with verses one, three, and six being sung from the shepherds' point of view, and verses two, four, and seven being sung from the perspective of the women in Bethlehem. Both groups sing verses five and eight.

The French text was roughly translated into English in 1862 by English Catholic bishop James Chadwick. He pared down the text to four stanzas and called it simply "Christmas Hymn." The complete song first appeared in English in a Methodist hymnal through a play called *The Nativity*. It used the same "Gloria" melody that is traditionally sung today and was arranged by Edward Shippen Barnes.

Carol of the Bells

Scan this QR code to hear a musical performance of "Carol of the Bells"

About the Carol

The tune for this popular carol hails from Ukraine, but strangely enough, the original lyrics have nothing to do with Christmas. In 1916, choral director Oleksander Koshyts commissioned composer Mykola Leontovych to write a song for an upcoming Christmas concert. He requested that the song be based on a Ukrainian folk chant. Leontovych took the first four notes and storyline from a traditional folk melody and created the choral work "Shchedryk." The title comes from the Ukrainian word *shchedryj*, which means "bountiful."

The song's lyrics celebrate winter and tell the story of a swallow singing to the master of a house and telling him all the good things he will receive—wealth, good crops, and so on—in the new year. The completed choral piece was first performed in 1916 at Kiev University. Soon, it became tradition to sing the piece as a well-wishing song for the new year, which was celebrated in Ukraine on January 13.

Young people would go from house to house, singing this and other similar songs. The carolers were often rewarded with treats from the places they visited.

In 1919, the Ukrainian National Chorus began a tour of more than one thousand concerts all across Europe and North and South America, where they introduced "Shchedryk" to the world. They even performed it at Carnegie Hall in New York City in 1921.

The song's popularity in Ukraine, however, could not be sustained during the chaotic years that followed its composition. "Soon after 'Shchedryk' gained popularity among choirs in the Ukraine," author Ace Collins notes, "the royal family of Russia was overthrown, Lenin rose to power, and the war to end all wars brought the globe into chaotic destruction. The Ukraine, which had been a unique nation with a distinct identity and culture, all but disappeared."

More than a decade and a half later, Peter Wilhousky, an arranger for the NBC Symphony Orchestra in New York City, came across Leontovych's "Shchedryk" while looking for music the orchestra could perform at a Christmas concert. The melody reminded him of bells and so he arranged the music for an orchestra and re-wrote the lyrics. The new arrangement—"Carol of the Bells"—was copyrighted in 1936 and has enjoyed immense success ever since, having been rearranged and recorded in various formats more than 150 times.

5

Good
King Wenceslas

Lyrics

Good King Wenceslas looked out
on the Feast of Stephen,
when the snow lay round about,
deep, and crisp, and even;

Brightly shone the moon that night,
though the frost was cruel,
when a poor man came in sight,
gath'ring winter fuel.

"Hither, page, and stand by me,
if thou know'st it, telling,
yonder peasant, who is he,
where and what his dwelling?"

"Sire, he lives a good league hence,
underneath the mountain,

right against the forest fence,
by Saint Agnes' fountain."

"Bring me flesh and bring me wine,
bring me pine logs hither;
thou and I will see him dine,
when we bear them thither."

Page and monarch, forth they went,
forth they went together,
through the rude wind's wild lament,
and the bitter weather.

"Sire, the night is darker now,
and the wind blows stronger;
fails my heart, I know not how;
I can go no longer."

"Mark my footsteps good, my page;
tread thou in them boldly:
thou shalt find the winter's rage
freeze thy blood less coldly."

In his master's steps he trod,
where the snow lay dinted;
heat was in the very sod
which the Saint had printed.

Therefore, Christians all, be sure,
wealth or rank possessing,
ye who now will bless the poor
shall yourselves find blessing.

Scan this QR code to watch a musical performance of "Good King Wenceslas"

About the Carol

This hymn tells the miraculous story of a righteous king and his page boy who venture into the cold winter night to provide comfort and supplies to the poor. The servant boy follows in the footsteps of the good king and can feel heat rising from those footprints, keeping him from freezing.

The song is very loosely based on first-century nobleman Wenceslaus I, sometimes referred to as the Duke of Bohemia and also known as Václav the Good. Wenceslaus did not produce magical footprints that kept his servant warm, nor was he a king during his lifetime. He was, however, known for his kindness and was posthumously given regal dignity by the Holy Roman Emperor Otto I—hence the title King Wenceslaus.

His family converted to Christianity before his birth. His mother, the daughter of a pagan tribal chief, converted to Christianity before marrying his father, and his paternal grandparents were converted in the late ninth century. Although Wenceslaus had to practice his faith secretly for a time, he still became well known for his good deeds as a follower of Christ. It is said that at Christmastime Wenceslaus gave gold coins to his servants and soldiers and was always known for his generosity.

He became a martyr when he was killed by his own brother, Boleslaus the Cruel, on September 28, A.D. 935. Wenceslaus was canonized a saint with haste, and the date—September 28—is now remembered as St. Wenceslaus Day. Wenceslaus later became the patron saint of the Czech people, and St. Wenceslaus Day was named a national holiday in the Czech Republic in 2000. Legend says that if the Czech Republic is ever in danger, the statue of St. Wenceslaus in Wenceslaus Square in Prague will come to life to defend the country.

An early twelfth-century priest, Cosmas of Prague, wrote: "[Wenceslaus'] deeds I think you know better than I could tell you; for, as is read in his Passion, no one doubts that, rising every night from his noble bed, with bare feet and only one chamberlain, he went around to God's churches and gave alms generously to widows, orphans, those in prison and afflicted by every difficulty" (in *Hastening toward Prague*, 150).

The carol that bears Wenceslaus's name was written in 1853 by John Mason Neale. How it became associated with Christmas is rather interesting. Somewhat ironically, the thirteenth-century tune Neale chose to accompany the text—"*Tempus adest floridum*" ("It is time for flowering")—was originally written to praise spring. Additionally, Neale did not write the carol to celebrate Christmas but to honor Saint Stephen's Day, or the Feast of Stephen. Neale meant for the song to be a reminder of the power of Christian kindness and belief. Because he had read extensively about the life of St. Wenceslaus and was particularly moved by records of Wenceslaus's mission to the poor on the Feast of Stephen, he used the "King" to frame his story.

As the Feast of Stephen is celebrated on December 26, the second day of Christmas, the song naturally became associated with Christmas—which seems a very appropriate time to celebrate Christian kindness after all!

Far, Far Away on Judea's Plains

Lyrics

Far, far away on Judea's plains,
Shepherds of old heard the joyous strains:

Glory to God,
Glory to God,
Glory to God in the highest;
Peace on earth, goodwill to men;
Peace on earth, goodwill to men!

Sweet are these strains of redeeming love,
Message of mercy from heav'n above:

Glory to God,
Glory to God,
Glory to God in the highest;
Peace on earth, goodwill to men;
Peace on earth, goodwill to men!

Lord, with the angels we too would rejoice;
Help us to sing with the heart and voice:

Glory to God,
Glory to God,
Glory to God in the highest;
Peace on earth, goodwill to men;
Peace on earth, goodwill to men!

Hasten the time when, from ev'ry clime,
Men shall unite in the strains sublime:

Glory to God,
Glory to God,
Glory to God in the highest;
Peace on earth, goodwill to men;
Peace on earth, goodwill to men!

 Scan this QR code to watch a musical performance of "Far, Far Away on Judea's Plains"

About the Carol

This carol has the distinction of first being written by a member of The Church of Jesus Christ of Latter-day Saints, but then gaining popularity with other Christian denominations. In 1869, Erastus Snow, an Apostle of the Church of Jesus Christ, was in charge of what was called the "Cotton Mission" in St. George, Utah. The weather had been poor, and food supplies were dwindling. Elder

Snow wanted to do something special for those in his charge for the upcoming Christmas.

He enlisted the help of two men, a poet named Charles Walker and the St. George choirmaster, John Macfarlane, and commissioned them to write a special Christmas song. The two had been collaborating on other songs, and they set to work right away to fulfill the request.

Walker wrote some lyrics, but Macfarlane had difficulty coming up with music that fit them properly. One night, he woke up in the middle of the night with a melody and lyrics running through his head. He woke his wife Ann, asking her to work the pump on the family's three-octave pump organ while he played what he was hearing in his mind. In the morning, he took the song to Walker, and they both agreed that it was what they were looking for. Macfarlane offered to give Walker credit for the lyrics, but Walker declined, since none of the words were, in his estimation, ones he had come up with.

"Far, Far Away on Judea's Plains" was performed for the first time at a Christmas program in St. George, Utah, in 1869 and was first published in *The Juvenile Instructor* in December 1889. Four years after Macfarlane's death, it was added to the Church of Jesus Christ's hymnal. It has since been included in other Christian hymnals.

7

O Holy Night

Lyrics

O holy night! The stars are brightly shining;
it is the night of our dear Savior's birth!
Long lay the world in sin and error pining,
till He appeared and the soul felt its worth.

A thrill of hope, the weary world rejoices,
for yonder breaks a new and glorious morn.
Fall on your knees! O hear the angel voices.
O night divine! O night when Christ was born.
O night, O holy night, O night divine!

Led by the light of faith serenely beaming,
with glowing hearts by His cradle we stand.
So led by light of a star sweetly gleaming,
here came the wise men from Orient land.

The King of kings lay thus in lowly manger,
in all our trials born to be our friend!

He knows our need, to our weakness is no stranger,
behold your King! Before Him lowly bend!
Behold your King! Before Him lowly bend!

Truly He taught us to love one another;
His law is love and His gospel is peace.
Chains shall He break, for the slave is our brother;
and in His name all oppression shall cease.

Sweet hymns of joy in grateful chorus raise we,
let all within us praise His Holy name.
Christ is the Lord! O praise His name forever,
His power and glory evermore proclaim.
His power and glory evermore proclaim.

 Scan this QR code to hear a musical performance of "O Holy Night"

About the Carol

The story of this stunningly beautiful song begins in 1840s France in the small town of Roquemaure, where a local poet, Placide Cappeau, was asked to write a poem that could be set to music and performed for a Christmas Mass. Cappeau was not particularly religious, but he had studied for a time under Jesuit priests at the Collège

Royal in Avignon and turned to the words of Luke 2 for inspiration.

Through a mutual friend, Cappeau received an introduction to the renowned opera and ballet composer Adolphe Adam. Adam had received great acclaim in 1841 for the ballet *Giselle* and lent his talents more frequently to ballet and opera than to standalone works. However, he agreed to set the text to music, completely unaware that the piece he was working on would one day be his most famous work next to *Giselle*.

The song, first titled "*Minuit chrétiens*" ("Midnight, Christians") but later changed to "*Cantique de Noël*" ("A Song of Christmas"), was debuted by the opera singer Emily Laurey. (Conflicting contemporary sources list the date as either 1843 or 1847.) The song's impressive lyrics and stirring score spread quickly to surrounding communities and generated a fair bit of controversy as they did. Cappeau's lyrics depicted Jesus as a redresser of wrongs and a liberator and breaker of chains, a message that some in the state-run Catholic Church found rebellious. Additionally, Cappeau later distanced himself from both the Catholic Church and the song in order to support a growing socialist movement in the country. For a time, the song was banned by the French Catholic Church.

The French people loved it so much, however, that

they continued to perform the song in their homes, which eventually led to it being heard by the American minister and writer John Sullivan Dwight.

Penned by Dwight in 1855, the English translation is much milder in its rhetoric. Dwight, a native of Boston, Massachusetts, was a Unitarian minister and transcendentalist who participated in the communal Brook Farm experiment with a number of well-known scholars, authors, and religionists of the time, including Nathaniel Hawthorne, Ralph Waldo Emerson, and Louisa May Alcott's parents. He was a strong abolitionist, and the message about Christ breaking the chains of the captive resonated with his anti-slavery views. He translated and liberally adapted the lyrics, which were published in a magazine distributed throughout the United States during the Civil War. The song became deeply associated with the abolitionist movement in the North.

Its popularity continued through the decades. In 1906, it gained the distinction of being the first song ever broadcast over radio waves when Canadian radio pioneer Reginald Fessenden decided to play "O Holy Night" on his violin and broadcast it.

Today, it has been recorded and broadcast hundreds of times over, enjoying popularity on both sides of the Atlantic Ocean.

Ding Dong! Merrily on High

Lyrics

Ding dong! Merrily on high,
in heav'n the bells are ringing:
Ding dong! Verily the sky
is riv'n with angel singing.

Gloria, Hosanna in excelsis!
Gloria, Hosanna in excelsis!

E'en so here below, below,
let steeple bells be swungen,
and i-o, i-o, i-o,
by priest and people sungen.

Gloria, Hosanna in excelsis!
Gloria, Hosanna in excelsis!

Pray you, dutifully prime
your Matin chime, ye ringers;
may you beautifully rhyme
your Eve-time Song, ye singers:

Gloria, Hosanna in excelsis!
Gloria, Hosanna in excelsis!

 Scan this QR code to watch a musical performance of "Ding Dong! Merrily on High"

About the Carol

This carol in its current form was literally hundreds of years in the making. In sixteenth-century France, Thoinot Arbeau, under his pen name, Jehan Tabourot (an anagram of his name in Latin), included the tune in his *Orchésographie*, a volume of dance songs. Called "*Branle de l'Official*," the tune was an upbeat French dance.

Hundreds of miles away and 350 years later, an Anglican priest named George Ratcliffe Woodward set words to the tune and published it in *The Cambridge Carol-Book* in 1924. Woodward was fascinated with church bells, which undoubtedly drew him to Tabourot's tune. He was also a linguist who often translated carols into English from Greek, Latin, and German. His love of language frequently led him to include Latin phrases in English songs. "Ding dong! Merrily on High" employs this macaronic device by using the Latin phrase "*Gloria, Hosanna in excelsis!*" ("Glory, Hosanna in the highest!") as a refrain in each verse.

God Bless
the Master

Lyrics

Arrangement by Ralph Vaughn Williams (1950)

God bless the master of this house,
with happiness beside
where'er his body rides or walks
his God must be his guide
his God must be his guide.

God bless the mistress of this house
with gold chain on her breast
where'er her body sleeps or wakes,
Lord send her soul to rest,
Lord send her soul to rest.

God bless your house, your children too,
your cattle and your store,
the Lord increase you day by day
and send you more and more
and send you more and more.

*Abridged arrangement by English folk
group The Watersons (1977)*

God bless the master of this house
and send him long to reign;
wherever he walks, wherever he rides,
Lord Jesus be his guide.
Lord Jesus be his guide.

God bless the mistress of this house
with a gold chain round her breast;
amongst her friends and kindred
God send her soul to rest.
God send her soul to rest. . . .

God bless the ruler of this house
and send him long to reign,
and many a merry Christmas
we may live to see again.
We may live to see again.

Now I have said my carol
which I intend to do;
God bless us all both great and small
and send us a happy New Year.
And send us a happy New Year.

Scan this QR code to hear a musical
performance of "God Bless the Master"

About the Carol

The words to this carol come from a very old folk song, likely dating back to somewhere between A.D. 1550 and 1650. The carol was first printed in a collection called *Ancient Songs and Ballads.* It is related to "The Wassailers' Carol," which was sung by carolers who went around singing and sharing hot wassail.

The famous British composer Ralph Vaughan Williams brought the carol into prominence when he included his own arrangement of it in his 1950 cantata, *Folk Songs of the Four Seasons.* Williams wrote the cantata for women's voices and included four movements and a prologue. Each movement is devoted to one of the four seasons. The final movement—"Winter"—features this carol, along with "Children's Christmas Song," the "Wassail Song," and "In Bethlehem City."

In one collection where this song was recorded, it was given the following description: "A carol that is midway between a wassail and a hymn, so a link between pagan luck-wish and pious hope. The words were widespread on garlands and broadsides around 1850, and several versions have been collected in the Southern counties during the twentieth century (most recently by Bob Cooper at North Waltham, Hampshire). The Watersons' tune and words are close to the set found by Vaughan Williams in 1909 at Preston Candover, barely five miles from North Waltham. The song was much used as a Mummers' Salutation, sung as an overture in front of the houses at New Year before the mummers began their patter" (A. L. Lloyd, "God Bless the Master of This House").

In Dulci Jubilo
(In Sweet Rejoicing)

Lyrics

Robert Lucas de Pearsall translation (1837)

In dulci jubilo [In sweet rejoicing]
let us our homage shew:
our heart's joy reclineth
in *praesepio* [in a manger];
and like a bright star shineth
matris in gremio [in the mother's lap],
Alpha es et O [Thou art Alpha and Omega]!

O Jesu parvule [O tiny Jesus],
my heart is sore for Thee!
Hear me, I beseech Thee,
O puer optime [O best of boys];
my praying, let it reach Thee,
O princeps gloriae [Prince of glory].
Trahe me post te [draw me unto thee].

O patris caritas [O father's caring]!
O Nati lenitas [O newborn's mildness]!
Deeply were we stained
per nostra crimina [by our crimes]:
but Thou for us hast gained
coelorum gaudia [heavenly joy],
qualis gloria [O that we were there]!

Ubi sunt gaudia [where be joys],
if that they be not there?
There are angels singing
nova cantica [new songs];
and there the bells are ringing
in Regis curia [at the king's court].
O that we were there!

 Scan this QR code to hear a musical
performance of "In Dulci Jubilo"

About the Carol

The traditional carol "*In dulci jubilo*"—Latin for "in
sweet rejoicing"—has been in use since at least the fourteenth century and has influenced many great musicians,
including Johann Sebastian Bach and Franz Liszt, who
each borrowed the melody for use in some of their own
work.

The tune was first seen in a manuscript in Germany in the Leipzig University Library around A.D. 1400. Since then, it has been used by Catholics, Protestants, Lutherans, and other Christians throughout the world in various forms. A Catholic version written in Latin and German employs the macaronic device of switching back and forth between two languages within a single verse. A Protestant version contains only the German translation. An 1837 version translated by Robert Lucas de Parsall again uses the macaronic device, switching between Latin and English. A loose 1853 English translation—"Good Christian Men, Rejoice"—written by clergyman John Mason Neale, increased the song's visibility in the English-speaking world. German Catholics today still use it as a processional song on Christmas Eve. No matter the language, the song perfectly captures the joy experienced by those who draw closer to God and feel His redeeming power.

The carol is most often attributed to German-Dominican monk Heinrich Seuse (Henry Suso in English). Born in A.D. 1295, Seuse became a Dominican monk at age thirteen. Seuse was devout in his beliefs and actions, continuously seeking higher learning and access to the divine. It is said that he spent years at the beginning of his service to God punishing himself—making himself as uncomfortable as possible—in order to seek God's approval. He later explained that his actions were unnecessary and distracted him from feeling God's love. He wrote about visions from angels and often told the story of his spiritual life. One such story describes how heavenly messengers appeared to him, singing "*In dulci jubilo*":

"Now this same angel came up to the Servitor [Suso] right blithely, and said that God had sent them down to him, to bring him heavenly joys amid his sufferings; adding that he must cast off all his sorrows from his mind and bear them company, and that he must also dance with them in heavenly fashion. Then they drew the Servitor by the hand into the dance, and the youth began a joyous [song] about the infant Jesus, which runs thus: 'In dulci jubilo'" (*Life of Blessed Henry Suso*, 28).

Of course, we can't be certain that angels actually taught Seuse "*In dulci jubilo*." But the carol's lyrics and meter do, indeed, make one feel as if they are dancing with the angels. The joyous cadence remains, no matter the language. As such, the carol is likely to continue inspiring joy for generations to come.

11

Joy to the World

Lyrics

Joy to the world, the Lord is come!
Let earth receive her King;
let every heart prepare Him room,
and heaven and nature sing,
and heaven and nature sing,
and heaven, and heaven, and nature sing.

Joy to the world, the Savior reigns!
Let men their songs employ;
while fields and floods, rocks, hills, and plains
repeat the sounding joy,
repeat the sounding joy,
repeat, repeat the sounding joy.

No more let sins and sorrows grow,
nor thorns infest the ground;
He comes to make His blessings flow
far as the curse is found,

far as the curse is found,
far as, far as, the curse is found.

He rules the world with truth and grace,
and makes the nations prove
the glories of His righteousness,
and wonders of His love,
and wonders of His love,
and wonders, wonders, of His love.

Scan this QR code to watch a musical
performance of "Joy to the World"

About the Carol

The text to this beloved carol first appeared in Isaac
Watts's 1719 book *The Psalms of David: Imitated in the
Language of the New Testament and Apply'd to the Christian
State and Worship.* With the work, Watts sought to look
at the Psalms through the light of Jesus's teachings in the
New Testament. The book consisted of Watts's original
poems, based on his paraphrasing of the 150 psalms in
the Old Testament. This poem, "Joy to the World," was
inspired by Psalm 98, as was another poem, entitled "To
Our Almighty Maker God."

Watts wrote in the book's first edition that with the

two poems on Psalm 98, he hoped to "have fully exprest what I esteem to be the first and chief Sense of the Holy Scriptures" (in "Psalm 98: Joy to the World").

Reading Psalm 98:4–9 provides of sense of Watts's inspiration:

"Make a joyful noise unto the Lord, all the earth: make a loud noise, and rejoice, and sing praise.

"Sing unto the Lord with the harp; with the harp, and the voice of a psalm.

"With trumpets and sound of cornet make a joyful noise before the Lord, the King.

"Let the sea roar, and the fulness thereof; the world, and they that dwell therein.

"Let the floods clap their hands: let the hills be joyful together

"Before the Lord; for he cometh to judge the earth: with righteousness shall he judge the world, and the people with equity."

In Watts's original poem, the third verse speaks of a "curse," which the coming Christ will forgive as His "blessings flow." This is a reference to the Fall of humankind that came upon Adam and Eve when they ate the forbidden fruit in the Garden of Eden. Watts proclaims that Christ will redeem humankind from the Fall of Adam. Because the verse is not directly based on Psalm

98, it is sometimes left out of denominational hymnals and is thus not as familiar as the other three verses.

It would be more than a century before Watts's poem was set to music. In 1836, American musician Lowell Mason adapted a tune called "Antioch" and paired it with Watts's text. The tune was not original to Mason but had appeared several times between 1832 and 1833 in various collections. Mason and others felt the tune was either influenced or written by George Frederic Handel. Though there is no direct evidence of this, Mason attributed the tune to Handel, and many modern hymnals continue to as well. Regardless of the tune's origins, it goes without saying the hymn is truly a masterpiece that praises "the wonders of His love" with unbridled joy.

O Come, All Ye Faithful

Lyrics

O come, all ye faithful,
joyful and triumphant!
O come ye, O come ye, to Bethlehem.
Come and behold him,
born the King of angels;

O come, let us adore him,
O come, let us adore him,
O come, let us adore him,
Christ the Lord!

Sing, choirs of angels,
sing in exultation;
sing, all ye citizens of heaven above!
Glory to God,
all glory in the highest;

O come, let us adore him,
O come, let us adore him,

O come, let us adore him,
Christ the Lord!

Yea, Lord, we greet Thee,
born this happy morning;
Jesus, to thee be glory given.
Word of the Father,
now in flesh appearing;

O come, let us adore him,
O come, let us adore him,
O come, let us adore him,
Christ the Lord!

Scan this QR code to watch a musical
performance of "O Come, All Ye Faithful"

About the Carol

This carol is a song of hope, a call to believers to come
to the Savior, as indicated by its title, *"Adeste, Fideles,"*
Latin for "Come, you faithful ones." In English, we know
the song as "O Come, All Ye Faithful."

The identity of the hymn's composer is somewhat of
a mystery, with musicologists and historians attempting
to unravel the threads of ownership for well over two
hundred years. The hymn is most frequently attributed

to John Francis Wade, a Catholic layman who fled England for France amidst Jacobite unrest around 1731. Wade took sanctuary at the English College in Douai, a Catholic seminary, where he was a musical copyist for manuscripts. He carefully signed and dated his manuscripts, including seven dated between 1743 and 1761 that contain the hymn. The earliest of these appeared in *Cantus Diversi*, a collection of musical manuscripts prepared by Wade.

Through the years, other bits of evidence have pointed to English organist and composer John Reading—or possibly his son, also named John Reading—as the composer. Some have believed King John IV of Portugal, "The Musician King," could be the hymn's creator, as there is evidence that he had a version of the hymn in his vast musical library as early as the mid-1600s. A number of other names have been thrown into the mix throughout time, including English composers Thomas Arne and Vincent Novello.

Wade's earliest manuscript included four verses. In the nineteenth century, the French Catholic priest Jean François-Étienne Borderies wrote three additional verses in Latin. An anonymous fourth Latin verse was later added but is not often used today.

Dozens of English hymn writers translated the hymn

after its first appearance in print, but the version that took hold wasn't written until the mid-1800s, when Frederick Oakley, an English Catholic priest, translated the original four verses for use at Margaret Chapel, his London church. It was printed with some revisions in F. H. Murray's *Hymnal for Use in the English Church* in 1852. Some thirty years later, William Thomas Brooke's translation of the additional four verses was combined with Oakley's translation and printed in the English form that most closely matches present-day use.

13

Mitt Hjerte Alltid Vanker (My Heart Always Wanders)

Lyrics

NORWEGIAN

*Mitt hjerte alltid vanker
i Jesu Føderom,
dit samles mine tanker
i deres hovedsum.
Der er min lengsel hjemme,
der har min tro sin skatt;
Jeg kan aldri glemme,
velsignet julenatt.*

*Akk, kom, jeg vil opplukke
mitt hjerte, sjel og sinn,
med tusen lengselssukke:
kom, Jesus, dog her inn!*

Det er ei fremmed bolig,
Du har den selv jo kjøpt.
så skal du blive trolig
uti mitt hjerte svøpt.

Jeg vil med palmegrene
ditt hvilested bestrø.
For deg, for deg alene
Jeg leve vil og dø.
Kom, la min sjel dog finne
sin rette frydestund,
at du er født her inne,
i hjertets dype grunn!

ENGLISH

My heart always wanders
to where Jesus was born,
there gather my thoughts
and take on their true form.
My longing belongs there,
with the treasure of my faith;
I shall never forget you,
O blessed Christmas night.

Oh, come, and I will open
my heart and my mind,
and with longing sigh:
comest thou in, Jesus.
You bought it for yourself

so I will remain faithful,
with you here in my heart.

I'll gladly spread branches
of palms 'round your crib,
for you, for you alone,
will I live and will I die.
Come, let my soul find joy
in this moment of delight;
to see you born right here,
deep inside my loving heart.

Scan this QR code to hear a musical
performance of *"Mitt Hjerte Alltid Vanker"*

About the Carol

This breathtaking Christmas song hails from Scandinavia and is based on a hymn penned by Danish bishop Hans Adolph Brorson in the early 1700s. It was made famous in our day by the Norwegian singer Sissel in 1995. The title, *"Mitt hjerte alltid vanker,"* means "My heart always wanders," and the song describes someone being drawn to the Christ child's birthplace. The simple words and melody inspire listeners to let Christ into their hearts.

Brorson's poem first appeared in print in 1731 or 1732 and included eleven verses. Several Scandinavian composers set various verses to music in the years that followed. The most popular version—and the one referenced here—is from Danish composer and violinist Carl Nielsen, in collaboration on the harmonies with his student Paul Hellmuth. For the melody, Nielsen adapted a Norwegian version of a Swedish folk tune. The song was first published in 1919 in a Danish collection of hymns and spiritual songs. It eventually made its way to *The Danish Psalm Book,* which version includes nine of Brorson's original verses. The well-known version performed by Sissel includes verses 1, 10, and 11 of Brorson's original poem, paired with Nielsen's composition.

14

Of the Father's Love Begotten

Lyrics

Of the Father's love begotten
ere the worlds began to be,
He is Alpha and Omega,
He the Source, the Ending He,
of the things that are, that have been,
and that future years shall see,
evermore and evermore!

O that birth forever blessed,
when the virgin, full of grace,
by the Holy Ghost conceiving,
bore the Savior of our race;
and the babe, the world's Redeemer,
first revealed His sacred face,
evermore and evermore!

This is He whom heav'n-taught singers
sang of old with one accord,

whom the Scriptures of the prophets
promised in their faithful word;
now He shines, the long expected;
let creation praise its Lord,
evermore and evermore!

O ye heights of heav'n adore Him;
angel hosts, His praises sing;
all dominions, bow before Him,
and extol our God and King!
Let no tongue on earth be silent,
ev'ry voice in concert ring,
evermore and evermore!

Christ, to thee, with God the Father,
and, O Holy Ghost, to thee,
hymn and chant and high thanksgiving,
and unwearied praises be,
honor, glory, and dominion,
and eternal victory,
evermore and evermore!

 Scan this QR code to hear a musical performance of "Of the Father's Love Begotten"

About the Carol

It's likely that this carol (titled in some hymnals "Of the Father's Heart Begotten") is the oldest Christmas hymn still sung by congregations today, with beginnings going back to the Holy Roman Empire.

It didn't start out as a Christmas carol, of course. But its celebratory praise of the Savior made it easily slip into use at Christmastime in the mid-1800s. The text is based on the old Latin poem "*Corde natus ex parentis.*" Its author, the great Roman poet Aurelius Prudentius, likely penned the words in the late fourth or early fifth century. He included the work in his *Hymnus omnis horae* (in English, *A Hymn for All Hours*). The work was a collection of twelve hymns, one numbered for each hour of the day. "*Corde natus ex parentis*" was a "fighting hymn," written to fight against the heretical perspectives of the day. It presents a well-reasoned argument about the nature of God and Jesus Christ. Prudentius was also a lawyer, and the song's persuasive construction shows evidence of that.

In 1582, the ancient poem was paired with a plain-chant melody from medieval times called "*Divinum mysterium.*" The melody has been embellished over the years but dates back to the tenth century in manuscript form.

The most common English translation of the song

was written by John Mason Neal in 1851. He added the refrain "Evermore and evermore"—a fitting exclamation for a song that has been sung for hundreds and hundreds of years and will likely continue to echo through cathedral walls for hundreds more.

Lo, How a Rose E'er Blooming

Lyrics

Lo, how a Rose e'er blooming
from tender stem hath sprung!
Of Jesse's lineage coming,
as those of old have sung.
It came, a floweret bright,
amid the cold of winter,
when half spent was the night.

Isaiah 'twas foretold it,
the Rose I have in mind:
with Mary we behold it,
the Virgin Mother kind.
To show God's love aright,
she bore to men a Savior,
when half spent was the night.

O Flower, whose fragrance tender
with sweetness fills the air,

dispel in glorious splendor
the darkness everywhere.
True man yet very God,
from sin and death now save us,
and share our every load.

Scan this QR code to watch a musical performance of "Lo, How a Rose E'er Blooming"

About the Carol

This German hymn dates back to at least 1599, when the text was found in the Carthusian monastery of St. Alban in what is now Trier, Germany. Its original German title, "*Es ist ein Ros entsprungen*," means "A rose has sprung up." The author is unknown, as is the author's true inspiration for the song. This has caused some dispute throughout the centuries about the carol's precise meaning. One legend surrounding the song speaks of a monk who found a rose blooming in the snow on Christmas Eve. Roses—often considered the queen of all flowers—have been a symbol of Mary throughout the centuries, so the monk, according to legend, placed the rose in a vase near the altar to the Virgin Mary and wrote the verses in her honor.

Other Christian scholars, however, believe the "Rose" in the carol symbolizes Jesus Christ, who came from "Jesse's lineage." These scholars note the similarity between the German word for rose (*Ros*) and the Old High German word for twig (*Reis*) and point to Isaiah's prophecies of the coming of the Savior, particularly verses such as Isaiah 11:1—"And there shall come forth a rod out of the stem of Jesse, and a Branch shall grow out of his roots."

The most familiar harmonization of the hymn occurred only ten years after the text's discovery when German composer Michael Praetorius set the verses to music in 1609. The hymn quickly became popular, and worshippers in many European countries—especially Germany—began singing the carol during Advent, the period beginning four Sundays before Christmas. Today, the carol is often sung as part of the Advent wreath tradition, which also originated in Germany. This tradition involves lighting one of four candles in a wreath each Sunday during Advent and singing carols such as this in celebration.

The most common English translation of the lyrics includes just two stanzas and was written in 1894 by Theodore Baker, an American who received his doctorate in music at Leipzig Conservatory in Germany. A third stanza, found in many Protestant hymnals and included here, was translated into English by Harriet Reynolds Krauth Spaeth. This stanza is based on one of two German stanzas altered from the original by Friedrich Layriz, a Lutheran pastor and hymnologist. This third stanza focuses on Jesus Christ's ability to dispel darkness and ease our mortal burdens.

Hark! The Herald Angels Sing

Lyrics

Hark! The herald angels sing,
"Glory to the newborn King;
peace on earth and mercy mild,
God and sinners reconciled!"
Joyful, all ye nations rise,
join the triumph of the skies;
with th'angelic host proclaim,
"Christ is born in Bethlehem."

Hark! The herald angels sing,
"Glory to the newborn King!"

Christ by highest heaven adored;
Christ, the everlasting Lord;
late in time behold him come,
offspring of a virgin's womb.
Veiled in flesh, our Lord is He;
Savior through eternity,

pleased with us in flesh to dwell,
Jesus, our Emmanuel.

Hark! The herald angels sing,
"Glory to the newborn King!"

Hail the heaven-born Prince of Peace!
Hail the Sun of Righteousness!
Light and life to all he brings,
risen with healing in his wings.
Mild he lays his glory by,
born that man no more may die,
born to raise the sons of earth,
born to give them second birth.

Hark! The herald angels sing,
"Glory to the newborn King!"

Scan this QR code to watch a musical performance of "Hark! The Herald Angels Sing"

About the Carol

The words to this stirring hymn come from the pen of the great Protestant reformer Charles Wesley, whose brother John Wesley was the founder of Methodism. Charles is said to have written more than six thousand hymns in his life, which makes him likely the most prolific male hymn writer in history. (Only the blind American poetess Fanny Crosby, who wrote more than eight thousand hymns, has him beat.)

Both Wesley brothers sought to teach solid doctrinal truths to their followers, and they believed that hymns were an ideal way to teach those truths. They had a particular interest in reaching the poor and illiterate, who could not always read or have access to scriptural texts. Anyone could, however, listen to and sing hymns— hymns that, sung many times over, would find a place in the heart. Together, the Wesley brothers published a number of hymn collections, though the bulk of the work was comprised of Charles's verses. In the preface to one volume, John wrote: "As but a small part of these hymns is of my own composing, I do not think it inconsistent with modesty to declare . . . that no such hymn-book as this has yet been published in the English language. In what other publication . . . have you so distinct and full an account of scriptural Christianity? such a declaration of the heights and depths of religion?" (*Collection of Hymns*, 4).

It is said that Charles Wesley wrote the words to this carol after feeling inspired by the sound of London church bells ringing out on Christmas Day 1738. The poem first appeared in print the following year in

Wesley's *Hymns and Sacred Poems* with the title "Hymn for Christmas Day" and the opening line, "Hark, how the welkin rings / Glory to the King of Kings." (*Welkin* is another word for heaven.)

Fourteen years later, George Whitefield, leader of the Calvinist movement among Methodists, changed Wesley's opening couplet, removed two verses, and published the poem in *A Collection of Hymns for Social Worship*. At this point, the tune we associate with the carol today had yet to come into use. It's possible that churchgoers used the tune set to one of Wesley's other hymns, such as "Christ the Lord Is Risen Today."

More than one hundred years later, in 1855, English musician William Hayman Cummings took the text from Whitefield's compilation and combined it with music by the famous German composer and organist Felix Mendelssohn. Cummings had met Mendelssohn as a child and had sung under his direction in a choir. The tune comes from the second part of a four-part cantata Mendelssohn wrote for the Leipzig Gutenberg Festival to celebrate the four hundredth anniversary of Gutenberg's printing press. Ironically, Mendelssohn believed the music was decidedly secular and writing to his publishers claimed, "It will never do to sacred words" (in *Carols of Christmas*, 113).

Cummings, nonetheless, adapted Mendelssohn's rousing composition to Wesley's powerfully beautiful—and very sacred—lines, and the rest is history.

Among the most beautiful lines in the hymn is one that describes how Christ brings "light and life" "with healing in his wings." The latter phrase comes from Malachi 4:2: "But unto you that fear my name shall the Sun of righteousness arise with healing in his wings."

Indeed, the entire song is replete with images from the Bible. Several stanzas from Wesley's original poem that aren't sung with much frequency today expand the hymn's message of rejoicing that God and sinners will be reconciled:

> Come, Desire of Nations, come,
> fix in us thy humble home;
> rise, the woman's conqu'ring seed,
> bruise in us the serpent's head.
>
> Now display thy saving Pow'r,
> ruin'd nature now restore,
> now in mystic union join
> Thine to ours, and ours to Thine.
>
> Adam's likeness, Lord, efface,
> stamp thy Image in its place,
> second Adam from above,
> reinstate us in thy love.

Let us Thee, tho' lost, regain,
Thee, the Life, the Heav'nly Man:
O! to all Thyself impart,
form'd in each believing heart.

Away in a Manger

Lyrics

Away in a manger,
no crib for a bed,
the little Lord Jesus
laid down his sweet head.
The stars in the sky
looked down where he lay,
the little Lord Jesus,
asleep on the hay.

The cattle are lowing,
the baby awakes,
but little Lord Jesus,
no crying he makes;
I love thee, Lord Jesus,
look down from the sky
and stay by my cradle
till morning is nigh.

Be near me, Lord Jesus,
I ask thee to stay
close by me forever,
and love me, I pray;
Bless all the dear children
in thy tender care,
and fit us for heaven
to live with thee there.

Scan this QR code to hear a musical
performance of "Away in a Manger"

About the Carol

Although this American Christmas carol originally appeared in an American newspaper, the hymn was initially presented as a much older German hymn. "Away in a Manger" was first published in an 1882 issue of the Boston newspaper *The Congregationalist*. How and why the two-verse carol appeared in the form it did is somewhat of a mystery. The newspaper called the song "Luther's Cradle Hymn," and a note accompanying the article claimed it was a song German reformer Martin Luther (1483–1546) had written to sing to his own children. According to the article, German mothers still sang the tune to their children. Within a few years' time, at least three other New England–area newspapers reprinted the song with the same claim.

This was decidedly incorrect. No record of the song has been found in Luther's papers. And the earliest English version of the song is many years older than any German version found. Furthermore, the earliest German version is clearly a translation from English.

Perhaps the publisher of *The Congregationalist* simply included the note and song to help mark the anniversary of Luther's birth four hundred years earlier. Or perhaps the publisher wanted to retell the sweet story of a father writing a song for his son and just took some creative license in doing so. Martin Luther did, in fact, write a Christmas hymn for his son, Hans: "*Vom Himmel hoch da komm ich her*," which means, "From Heaven on High I Come to You."

In 1885, the song, still only two stanzas at this point, was printed in a hymnal for the first time. The Evangelical Lutheran church responsible for the collection—*Little Children's Book for School and Families*—knew the attribution to Luther could not be correct and therefore did not include it in the printing. They also changed the name to "Away in a Manger," reflecting the first few words of the song.

Several other composers included the song in collections in the years that followed, some getting the attribution correct, others not. In 1892, Charles H. Gabriel printed an arrangement of the hymn that included a third verse. Gabriel again attributed the song to Luther, but dropped his name from the title, simply calling it "Cradle Song." The writer of that third verse is also unknown.

More than forty different tunes have accompanied the song since its first printing. The two that remain most common today are William Kirkpatrick's 1895 tune "Cradle Song" and James R. Murray's 1887 tune "Mueller," which Murray named after the German composer Carl Mueller.

Angels from the Realms of Glory

Lyrics

Angels from the realms of glory,
wing your flight o'er all the earth;
ye who sang creation's story
now proclaim Messiah's birth.

Come and worship, come and worship,
worship Christ, the newborn King.

Shepherds, in the field abiding,
watching o'er your flocks by night,
God with us is now residing;
yonder shines the infant light:

Come and worship, come and worship,
worship Christ, the newborn King.

Sages, leave your contemplations,
brighter visions beam afar;

seek the great Desire of nations;
ye have seen His natal star.

Come and worship, come and worship,
worship Christ, the newborn King.

Saints, before the altar bending,
watching long in hope and fear;
suddenly the Lord, descending,
in His temple shall appear.

Come and worship, come and worship,
worship Christ, the newborn King.

Sinners, wrung with true repentance,
doomed for guilt to endless pains,
justice now revokes the sentence,
mercy calls you—break your chains.

Come and worship, come and worship,
worship Christ, the newborn King.

Though an infant now we view him,
he shall fill his Father's throne,
gather all the nations to him;
every knee shall then bow down:

Come and worship, come and worship,
worship Christ, the newborn King.

Scan this QR code to watch a musical performance of "Angels from the Realms of Glory"

About the Carol

James Montgomery was born in Scotland in 1771 to devoutly Protestant parents who were pioneers of the Moravian Church movement in Scotland. At age six, he was sent to study with the Moravian Brethren in a small town near Leeds, England. Two of his brothers joined him there six years later when their parents left for the West Indies to become missionaries. This reunion was the last time James would see his parents. His mother died on Tobago in 1790, and his father the following year in Barbados.

James did not particularly enjoy his studies at the school and had little desire to follow his parents' path into the Moravian ministry. His years at the school were lonely and somewhat troubled. Despite this, he began writing poetry when he had time and even managed to sell some around town during a transitionary period between his time at the school and a complete break with the Brethren, who were considered his legal guardians in his parents' absence. At seventeen, Montgomery was legally free to do and live as he pleased. He hopped from small job to small job, continuing to write and submit poems to publishers in his free time. He eventually found steady work a few years later at a newspaper in Sheffield titled *Iris*—a newspaper he would end up running himself for more than thirty years—when the original owner/editor was forced to flee to America due to his liberal views and agitation for parliamentary reform.

The "new" paper had a bumpy start, which almost immediately included a three-month stint in prison for Montgomery on charges of printing seditious libel against the king. The "libel" was a patriotic song Montgomery agreed to print because the type had been set before the former editor left and because Montgomery felt printing it to be an act of charity for the poor street monger who had written the ballad.

Eventually, Montgomery and the paper found their pace. With the time and means to publish his own work, Montgomery began writing more often. His most well-known writings were hymns, including "Prayer Is the Soul's Sincere Desire," "A Poor Wayfaring Man of Grief," and "The Lord Is My Shepherd," which he based on the 23rd Psalm. Montgomery published "Angels from the Realms of Glory" in his newspaper on Christmas Eve, 1816.

The lyrics are inspired by the Nativity story from Luke 2, with each stanza in the poem addressing a different group: the angels, the shepherds, the Magi, saints and sinners (each in a separate stanza), and finally, all the nations of the world.

In the United States, the hymn is most often set to the tune "Regent Square" by the great British organist Henry Smart. In England, however, the song is primarily sung to an old French folk tune now called "Iris," after the name of Montgomery's newspaper. That tune is very similar to the tune used for "Angels We Have Heard on High."

December
19

Masters
in This Hall

Lyrics

Masters in this Hall,
hear ye news to-day
brought from over sea,
and ever I you pray:

Nowell! Nowell! Nowell!
Sing we clear!
Holpen are all folk on earth
Born is God's Son so dear!

Then to Bethl'em town
went we two and two,
and in a sorry place
heard the oxen low:

Nowell! Nowell! Nowell!
Sing we clear!
Holpen are all folk on earth
Born is God's Son so dear!

Ox and ass Him know,
kneeling on their knee:
wonderous joy had I
this little Babe to see.

Nowell! Nowell! Nowell!
Sing we clear!
Holpen are all folk on earth
Born is God's Son so dear!

This is Christ the Lord,
masters, be ye glad!
Christmas is come in,
and no folk shall be sad!

Nowell! Nowell! Nowell!
Sing we clear!
Holpen are all folk on earth
Born is God's Son so dear!

Scan this QR code to hear a musical
performance of "Masters in This Hall"

About the Carol

This is a simple carol set to an old French dance tune.
The text, written by English poet William Morris around
1860, is presented as an announcement of the Savior's
birth. That announcement, however, is not from angels

on high but from humble peasant folk who have run to their wealthy masters to share the wonderful news. The tune evokes their merriment and a celebratory mood. The full poem hints at the Savior's teachings that the meek "shall inherit the earth" (Matthew 5:5) and the proud shall be as stubble (see Malachi 4:1).

Though the song has never gained status as a famous Christmas carol, it is still used throughout the world and is quite popular with choral groups at high schools and universities, especially in madrigal competitions.

Morris's original poem included twelve verses, but only four or five are typically sung today. The tune Morris chose to accompany his text is "*Marche pour les Matelots.*" The tune was originally written for *Alcyone,* an opera composed by Marin Marais. It was subsequently published in several dance collections in the early 1700s.

O du Fröhliche
(O You Joyful)

Lyrics

GERMAN

O du fröhliche, o du selige,
Gnadenbringende Weihnachtszeit!
Welt ging verloren, Christ ist geboren:
Freue, freue dich, o Christenheit!

O du fröhliche, o du selige,
Gnadenbringende Weihnachtszeit!
Christ ist erschienen, uns zu versöhnen:
Freue, freue dich, o Christenheit!

O du fröhliche, o du selige,
Gnadenbringende Weihnachtszeit!
Himmlische Heere jauchzen Dir Ehre:
Freue, freue dich, o Christenheit!

O you joyful, O you blessed,
grace-bringing Christmas time!
The world was lost, Christ is born:
rejoice, rejoice, O Christendom!

O you joyful, O you blessed,
grace-bringing Christmas time!
Christ appeared to atone for us:
rejoice, rejoice, O Christendom!

O you joyful, O you blessed,
grace-bringing Christmas time!
Heavenly armies rejoice in your hour:
rejoice, rejoice, O Christendom!

Scan this QR code to hear a musical
performance of *"O du Fröhliche"*

About the Carol

This popular German carol ("O You Joyful" in English) first appeared in 1816 under one of the longest one-word titles you may have ever seen: *"Allerdreifeiertagslied."* The word roughly means "A Song for Three Holidays," the holidays being Christmas, Easter, and Pentecost. The original text included one verse about each holiday and was penned by Johannes Daniel Falk, a poet and publisher living in Weimar, Germany, at the time. Falk set the words to the Catholic tune "*O Sanctissima*," which means "O Most Holy." The anonymous tune dates back to 1792 and is sometimes called "The Sicilian Mariners' Hymn."

Falk had lofty ideals in every part of his life. As a writer, he associated with both Goethe and Schiller. As a businessman, he worked to help those in need, founding an orphanage in Weimar where abandoned children could live and study. It is said that Falk helped more than five hundred orphans from around Weimar and was often called the "Father of Orphans." He dedicated "*Allerdreifeiertagslied*" to the children of the orphanage. Having lost four of his own children to typhoid fever, the children of the orphanage were very dear to him and he took great delight in hearing them—his "own" orphan children—sing "*Allerdreifeiertagslied.*"

After Falk's death, his assistant, Heinrich Holzschuher, adapted the song to be suitable for one holiday instead of three: Christmas. Holzschuher kept the first verse as is and modified the second two so they spoke of Christmas instead of Easter or Pentecost.

Today, the song remains immensely popular in Germany and is often sung at the end of Protestant Christmas Eve services throughout the country.

December

21

In the Bleak Midwinter

Lyrics

In the bleak midwinter,
frosty wind made moan,
earth stood hard as iron,
water like a stone.
Snow had fallen,
snow on snow, snow on snow,
in the bleak midwinter,
long ago.

Our God,
heaven cannot hold him,
nor earth sustain;
heaven and earth shall flee away
when He comes to reign.
In the bleak midwinter
a stable place sufficed

the Lord God Almighty,
Jesus Christ.

Angels and archangels
may have gathered there,
cherubim and seraphim
thronged the air.
But his mother only,
in her maiden bliss
worshiped the beloved
with a kiss.

What can I give him,
poor as I am?
If I were a shepherd,
I would bring a lamb;
if I were a Wise Man,
I would do my part;
yet what I can I give him:
give my heart.

 Scan this QR code to watch a musical
performance of "In the Bleak Midwinter"

About the Carol

This poem's beautiful message focuses on not only
what the Savior gave to each of us, but also on what we

can offer Him in return—the gift of our hearts. From what we know of the poet's life, it appears she, herself, offered up her heart through poetry, art, and dedicated service to others. Christina Rossetti was born in 1830 to Italian parents living in exile in London, England.

Throughout her life, she was surrounded by proponents of art, literature, and the continual seeking of knowledge. Her father, Gabriele, was a professor of Italian at King's College in London. Her brothers, Dante and William, were well-known artists who helped found the prominent Pre-Raphaelite Brotherhood, a famous art community in England. Christina was a personal friend of Charles Dodgson, the author of *Alice's Adventures in Wonderland* and *Through the Looking-Glass* under the pen name of Lewis Carroll.

Rossetti devoted herself to writing, the arts, and acts of Christian service, and, having turned down two marriage proposals, she was sometimes called a "nun of art."

During her life, she published several collections of poetry, much of it religious. "In the Bleak Midwinter" was originally written as a poem and published in the January 1872 issue of *Scribner's Monthly*. The editor of the magazine had reached out to her to request a Christmas poem. There, it appeared under the title "A Christmas

Carol." But it did not, in fact, become a Christmas carol until after Rossetti's death.

In 1906, her words were paired with a tune by Gustav Holst for publication in *The English Hymnal*. There, the carol was given the title "In the Bleak Midwinter." Today, Rossetti is considered one of the most important poets of the nineteenth century, and her influence has stretched into the twenty-first century. In 2008, *BBC Music* magazine listed "In the Bleak Midwinter" as the best Christmas carol, according to leading choral directors and choirmasters in England and the United States.

December

22

The First Noel

Lyrics

The first Noel the angel did say
was to certain poor shepherds in fields as they lay;
in fields where they lay keeping their sheep,
on a cold winter's night that was so deep.

Noel, Noel, Noel, Noel,
born is the King of Israel!

They looked up and saw a star
shining in the east, beyond them far;
and to the earth it gave great light,
and so it continued both day and night.

Noel, Noel, Noel, Noel,
born is the King of Israel!

And by the light of that same star
three Wise Men came from country far;

to seek for a king was their intent,
and to follow the star wherever it went.

Noel, Noel, Noel, Noel,
born is the King of Israel!

This star drew nigh to the northwest,
o'er Bethlehem it took its rest;
and there it did both stop and stay,
right over the place where Jesus lay.

Noel, Noel, Noel, Noel,
born is the King of Israel!

Then entered in those Wise Men three,
full reverently upon the knee,
and offered there, in his presence,
their gold and myrrh and frankincense.

Noel, Noel, Noel, Noel,
born is the King of Israel!

Then let us all with one accord
sing praises to our heavenly Lord,
that He this glorious earth hath wrought
and with His blood mankind hath bought.

Noel, Noel, Noel, Noel,
born is the King of Israel!

Scan this QR code to watch a musical
performance of "The First Noel"

About the Carol

In medieval times, congregational participation in Mass was rare. Regular townsfolk didn't meet inside the church, but outside on the streets. The people shared stories and tunes with one another, using humble words and melodies that differed vastly from the high church hymns being sung inside. They passed down songs for Easter celebrations, for Epiphany, and for celebration of the Savior's birth—doing so preserved, in their own words, the stories important to their faith. These gatherings are often where folk carols like "The First Noel" had their beginnings. Indeed, historians think it's likely that the melody and lyrics for this Epiphany carol were passed down through oral tradition for hundreds of years before the words first appeared in print on broadsides in a small village near Cornwall, England, around 1816.

Nine stanzas from the poem appeared again in 1823, this time in Davies Gilbert's anthology, *Some Ancient Christmas Carols*. Gilbert was a Cornish author and politician who hoped to reintroduce Christmas carols—and the practice of singing them—in England. In 1833, William Sandys, a collector of Christmas carols, took the poem as it appeared in Gilbert's anthology and paired it with music. The carol was printed in his collection, *Christmas*

Carols, Ancient and Modern. The version Sandys included is somewhat of an anomaly, as it seems to be a blend of various other tunes, with some folklorists speculating that some phrases of the passed-down tune were not the original melody but notes that would have been sung in the tenor voice. William Stainer, a popular English composer, standardized the tune some years later for use in Sandys's new 1876 collection, *Christmas Carols Old and New.*

In the years that followed, other folklorists discovered different variations of the tune and lyrics, evidence that the carol had changed here and there as it was passed down through the years. The English folksong collector Cecil Sharp discovered a version in 1914, noting that it was "sung by Mr. Bartle Symons, who learnt it many years ago from Mr. Spago (70 or 80 years of age)."

Whether the carol is of French or English origin is up for some debate. Cornwall is just across the English Channel from France, so it's thought that the carol may have migrated from France despite its first being published in the English language. Whatever its beginnings, this humble song—created by people who likely couldn't read scriptural text but hoped to preserve the stories of their faith in other ways—is now beloved the world over, sung both inside and outside of great cathedrals everywhere.

Infant Holy, Infant Lowly

Lyrics

Infant holy, infant lowly,
for his bed a cattle stall;
oxen lowing, little knowing,
Christ the Babe is Lord of all.
Swiftly are winging angels singing,
Noels ringing, tidings bringing:
Christ the Babe is Lord of all.

Flocks were sleeping, shepherds keeping
vigil till the morning new
saw the glory, heard the story,
tidings of a gospel true.
Thus rejoicing, free from sorrow,
praises voicing, greet the morrow:
Christ the Babe was born for you!

Scan this QR code to watch a musical performance of "Infant Holy, Infant Lowly"

About the Carol

While many English, French, and German carols have entered the American Christmas tradition, few from Eastern Europe have made it here. This carol is one of those few. Its Polish title, "*W Żłobie Leży,*" means "In a Manger Lies." It is thought to be an old Polish folk carol, possibly dating back to the thirteenth or fourteenth century.

Edith Margaret Reed, editor of the English magazine *Music and Youth,* found "*W Żłobie Leży*" in a 1908 compilation of Polish Christmas carols. She worked on an English translation of the carol that would retain the simple phrasing and tight rhymes present in the original Polish. The result was "Infant Holy, Infant Lowly," a beautiful, almost haunting, carol set at the scene of the manger where the Christ child was born. It was printed for the first time in 1921 in Reed's *Music and Youth* magazine.

In 1930, American poet and teacher Nancy Byrd Turner used "*W Żłobie Leży*" with her own poem "Stars Were Gleaming" and published the piece in a collection of hymns for children. Turner wrote poetry for people of all ages but was particularly interested in writing poetry and lyrics for children. Her poems were widely published in *Harper's Magazine, The Atlantic,* and the *New Yorker,* among others. Her lyrics are a children's retelling of the Nativity:

> Stars were gleaming, shepherds dreaming;
> And the night was dark and chill.
> Angels' story, rang with glory;
> Shepherds heard it on the hill.
> Ah, that singing! Hear it ringing,
> Earthward winging, Christmas bringing.
> Hearken! We can hear it still!
>
> See the clearness and the nearness
> Of the blessed Christmas star,
> Leading, guiding; wise men riding
> Through the desert dark and far.
> Lovely showing, shining growing,
> Onward going, gleaming glowing,
> Leading still, our Christmas Star!

Stille Nacht
(Silent Night)

Lyrics

GERMAN

Stille Nacht, heilige Nacht
Alles schläft; einsam wacht
Nur das traute hochheilige Paar.
Holder Knabe im lockigen Haar,
Schlaf in himmlischer Ruh!
Schlaf in himmlischer Ruh!

Stille Nacht, heilige Nacht,
Hirten erst kundgemacht
Durch der Engel Halleluja,
Tönt es laut von fern und nah:
Christ, der Retter ist da!
Christ, der Retter ist da!

Stille Nacht, heilige Nacht,
Gottes Sohn, o wie lacht

Lieb aus deinem göttlichen Mund,
Da uns schlägt die rettende Stund,
Christ, in deiner Geburt!
Christ, in deiner Geburt!

ENGLISH

Silent night, holy night,
All is calm, all is bright
Round yon virgin mother and child.
Holy infant, so tender and mild,
Sleep in heavenly peace,
Sleep in heavenly peace.

Silent night, holy night,
Shepherds quake at the sight;
Glories stream from heaven afar,
Heavenly hosts sing, Alleluia!
Christ the Savior is born,
Christ the Savior is born!

Silent night, holy night,
Son of God, love's pure light;
Radiant beams from thy holy face,
With the dawn of redeeming grace,
Jesus, Lord, at thy birth,
Jesus, Lord, at thy birth.

Scan this QR code to hear a musical
performance of "Silent Night"

About the Carol

"*Stille Nacht*"—or "Silent Night" in English—is one of the most well-known and well-loved Christmas carols of all time.

The text comes from a young Austrian priest, Joseph Mohr, born in 1792 in Salzburg. Mohr grew up under the tutelage of the vicar and leader of music at Salzburg Cathedral, Johann Nepomuk Hiernle. At the cathedral, he gained both an education and a love for music. He later studied at the Benedictine monastery of Kremsmünster and played the violin and sang in the choirs at two different churches.

Mohr wrote the words to "*Stille Nacht*" in 1816. Two years later, on Christmas Eve morning, he brought the poem to Franz Gruber, the organist at the St. Nicholas Church in Oberndorf, where Mohr was serving as assistant priest. He hoped Gruber could come up with a melody for the song so it could be performed that night at Christmas Eve Mass. Gruber proved up to the task. That night, the two performed "*Stille Nacht*" for the first time. Mohr sang the tenor part, while also accompanying the song on his guitar. Gruber provided the bass part.

It is not known why the two chose to use the guitar instead of the organ. Some historians have suggested that the organ was out of commission, but there is no indication that was the case. Gruber himself wrote in detail about the hymn and its creation but never mentioned a problem with the organ.

The song's original arrangement included six verses to be sung by two voices with choral and guitar accompaniment. The last two lines of each verse were to be repeated by the choir in four-part harmony.

In the 1830s, the song caught the attention of two Austrian performing families, the Strasser siblings and the Rainer family. Like the Von Trapp Family Singers of *The Sound of Music* fame, the two families traveled across Europe singing and performing. They incorporated the tune into their programs, where it quickly became universally loved.

During this time, the melody of the song evolved somewhat, with a few notes being dropped here and there, until it became what we recognize today. The American Episcopal priest John Freeman Young translated three of Mohr's verses into English in 1859 and published them in a pamphlet titled *Carols for Christmas*. It didn't take long before the song gained popularity in the States. In the years since, more than three hundred translations of the song have been made in more than one hundred and fifty different languages. Hallein, Austria, just outside of Salzburg, is home to an entire museum dedicated to the song: *Stille Nacht* Museum.

In 1914, just a few months into the First World War, Pope Benedict XV called for a Christmas cease-fire. His plea was rejected by wartime officials, but a battlefield truce occurred nonetheless. For two days—Christmas Eve and Christmas Day 1914—soldiers from both sides of the war left the trenches on the Western Front and joined together in song and sport. Soldiers on both sides sang the peaceful strains of "Silent Night" in their native languages—German, French, and English—simultaneously. For a moment, a song united men who understood neither the language nor the motivations of their enemies.

Today, *Stille Nacht* is considered the most sacred of all Christmas carols in Germany and Austria. It cannot be used in any commercial context in these countries, and it is typically only sung on Christmas Eve, just as it was in a small church in Austria more than two hundred years ago.

Bibliography

The Holly and the Ivy

Judith Ellis, "The Holly and the Ivy," *Chipping Campden History Society* (website); available at https://www.chippingcampdenhistory.org.uk /content/archives/from-the-archives/the-holly-and-the-ivy; accessed 13 December 2021.

"The Holly and the Ivy," in *The New Oxford Book of Carols,* Hugh Keyte and Andrew Parrot, eds. (Oxford: Oxford University Press, 1992), 436–37.

Mark Lawson-Jones, *Why Was the Partridge in the Pear Tree? The History of Christmas Carols (Gloucestershire, UK: History Press, 2011),* 69–75.

Mormon Tabernacle Choir, *Let the Season In* (music CD; 2014).

O Little Town of Bethlehem

Alexander V. G. Allen, *Life and Letters of Phillips Brooks, Volume 1* (New York: E. P. Dutton, 1900), 573.

———, *Phillips Brooks, 1835–1893: Memories of His Life with Extracts from His Letters and Note-Books* (New York: E. P. Dutton, 1907), 577.

"The Brahmin Celebrity Priest Who Wrote O Little Town of Bethlehem," *New England Historical Society* (website); available at https://www .newenglandhistoricalsociety.com/the-brahmin-celebrity-priest-who -wrote-o-little-town-of-bethlehem; accessed 10 December 2021.

Phillips Brooks, "O Little Town of Bethlehem," *The United Methodist*

Hymnal: Book of United Methodist Worship (Nashville: United Methodist Publishing, 1989), 230b.

Andrew Gant, *The Carols of Christmas: A Celebration of Surprising Stories behind Your Favorite Hymns* (Nashville: Nelson Books, 2015), 38–46.

Mormon Tabernacle Choir, *Merry Christmas with the Mormon Tabernacle Choir* (music CD; 2015).

Angels We Have Heard on High

"Angels We Have Heard on High," *United Methodist Hymnal,* 238.

Adrian Fortescue, "Gloria in Excelsis Deo," in *The Catholic Encyclopedia, Volume 6* (New York: Encyclopedia Press, 1913), 581–86.

C. Michael Hawn and Jeanne Larson Williams, "History of Hymns: 'Angels We Have Heard on High,'" Mississippi Conference of The United Methodist Church, 22 December 2015; available at https://www.mississippi-umc.org/newsdetail/history-of-hymns-angels-we-have-heard-on-high-3216478; accessed 10 December 2021.

Mormon Tabernacle Choir, *Merry Christmas with the Mormon Tabernacle Choir* (music CD; 2015).

Carol of the Bells

B. J. Almond, "'Carol of the Bells' wasn't originally a Christmas song," press release, Rice University News and Media Relations Office of Public Affairs, 13 December 2004; available at https://news.rice.edu/2004/12/13/carol-of-the-bells-wasnt-originally-a-christmas-song/; accessed 10 December 2021.

Ace Collins, *Stories behind the Greatest Hits of Christmas* (Grand Rapids, MI: Zondervan, 2010), 38–42.

Mormon Tabernacle Choir, *The Wonder of Christmas* (music CD; 2006).

Good King Wenceslas

Andrew Gant, *Carols of Christmas,* 136–42.

"Good King Wenceslas," *Complete Anglican Hymns Old and New,* Susan Sayers and Michael Forster, eds. (Suffolk, UK: Kevin Mayhew Ltd., 2000), 370.

Mark Lawson-Jones, *Why Was the Partridge in the Pear Tree?* 113–21.

Francis Mershman, "Wenceslas," in *The Catholic Encyclopedia, Volume 15* (New York: Encyclopedia Press, 1913), 587.

Mormon Tabernacle Choir, *Once Upon a Christmas* (music CD; 2012).

Lisa Wolverton, *Hastening toward Prague: Power and Society in the Medieval Czech Lands* (Philadelphia: University of Pennsylvania Press, 2001).

Far, Far Away on Judea's Plains

Lyman Hafen, *A Dixie Christmas* (St. George, UT: Publisher's Place, 1988).

Mormon Tabernacle Choir, *Let the Season In* (music CD; 2017).

Ardis Parshall, "John Menzies Macfarlane: Far, Far Away and Not So Long Ago," *Keepapitchinin.org* (website); available at http://www .keepapitchinin.org/2008/12/14/john-menzies-macfarlane-far-far -away-and-not-so-long-ago/; accessed 24 March 2022.

Washington County Historical Society (website); available at https://wchs utah.org/entertainment/far-far-away.php; accessed 24 March 2022.

O Holy Night

Andrew Gant, *Carols of Christmas,* 76–88.

Benjamin Ivry, "A brief history of 'O Holy Night,' the rousing Christmas hymn that garnered mixed reviews," *America: The Jesuit Review* (website), 19 November 2020; available at https://www.americamagazine .org/arts-culture/2020/11/19/brief-history-o-holy-night-christmas -hymn-review; accessed 10 December 2021.

Dale V. Nobbman, *Christmas Music Companion Fact Book* (Anaheim Hills: Centerstream Publishing, 2000), 36.

The Tabernacle Choir at Temple Square, *Christmas Best* (music CD; 2021).

Ding Dong! Merrily on High

Andrew Gant, *Carols of Christmas,* 90–95.

Mormon Tabernacle Choir, *Rejoice and Be Merry!* (music CD; 2008).

George Ratcliffe Woodward, "Ding Dong! Merrily on High," *Hymns and Carols of Christmas* (website); available at https://www.hymns

andcarolsofchristmas.com/Hymns_and_Carols/Images/Woodward -Cambridge/007-b.jpg; accessed 10 December 2021.

God Bless the Master

"Folk Songs of the Four Seasons," *The Ralph Vaughn Williams Society* (website); available at https://rvwsociety.com/folk-songs-four-seasons/; accessed 13 December 2021.

A. L. Lloyd, "God Bless the Master of This House," *Mainly Norfolk: English Folk and Other Good Music* (website); available at https://mainlynorfolk.info/watersons/songs/godblessthemaster.html; accessed 13 December 2021.

Mormon Tabernacle Choir, *Home for the Holidays* (music CD; 2015).

In Dulci Jubilo (In Sweet Rejoicing)

Doug Anderson, "Notes to *In Dulci Jubilo*," *The Hymns and Carols of Christmas* (website); available at http://www.hymnsandcarolsof christmas.com/Hymns_and_Carols/Notes_On_Carols/in_dulci _jubilo.htm; accessed 13 December 2021.

Andrew Gant, *Carols of Christmas,* 48–55.

"A German Christmas Carol in Latin, German and English," *The German Way & More* (website); available at https://www.german-way.com /history-and-culture/german-language/german-christmas-carols /in-dulci-jubilo/; accessed 13 December 2021.

"*In dulci jubilo:* Good Christian men, rejoice!" in *New Oxford Book of Carols,* 193–98.

Henry Suso, *The Life of Blessed Henry Suso by Himself,* translated by Thomas Francis Knox (London: Burns, Lambert, and Oates, 1865).

The Tabernacle Choir at Temple Square, *Christmas Day in the Morning* (music CD; 2020).

Joy to the World

Chris Fenner, "Psalm 98: Joy to the World," *Hymnology Archive* (website), 13 December 2018; available at https://www.hymnologyarchive .com/joy-to-the-world; accessed 13 December 2021.

"History of Hymns: 'Joy to the World,'" *Discipleship Ministries of The*

United Methodist Church (website), December 22, 2015; available at https://www.umcdiscipleship.org/resources/history-of-hymns-joy-to-the-world; accessed 13 December 2021.

"Joy to the World," in *New Oxford Book of Carols,* 270–74.

Mormon Tabernacle Choir, *A Merry Little Christmas* (music CD; 2018).

Isaac Watts, "Joy to the World," *United Methodist Hymnal,* 246.

———, *The Psalms of David: Imitated in the Language of the New Testament and Apply'd to the Christian State and Worship,* second edition (London, 1719), 201.

O Come, All Ye Faithful

"*Adeste Fideles,*" in *New Oxford Book of Carols*, 238–43.

Andrew Gant, *Carols of Christmas,* 56–66.

C. Michael Hawn, "History of Hymns: 'O Come, All Ye Faithful,'" *Discipleship Ministries of The United Methodist Church* (website), 20 May 2013; available at https://www.umcdiscipleship.org/resources/history-of-hymns-o-come-all-ye-faithful; accessed 13 December 2021.

Mark Lawson-Jones, *Why Was the Partridge in the Pear Tree?* 82–95.

Mormon Tabernacle Choir, *Hallelujah!* (music CD; 2016).

John Stephan, "*Adeste Fideles:* A Study on Its Origin and Development" (Buckfast Abbey, South Devon, 1947); available at http://www.hymnsandcarolsofchristmas.com/Hymns_and_Carols/Images/Stephan/adeste_fideles_a_study_on_its_or.htm; accessed 13 December 2021.

Mitt Hjerte Alltid Vanker (My Heart Always Wanders)

Ragnhild Helena Aadland Høen, "The Story behind 'My Heart Always [Wanders],'" *Norwegian Choir Association* (website), 23 December 2019; available at https://korbloggen.no/historien-bak-mitt-hjerte-alltid-vanker/; accessed 13 December 2021.

Lisbeth Larsen, "Wonderful to Say," *The Royal Library, Denmark* (website), 2009; available at http://www5.kb.dk/da/nb/samling/ma/fokus/mdrsang/cnforunderligt.html; accessed 13 December 2021.

Mormon Tabernacle Choir, *Spirit of the Season* (music CD; 2017).

Of the Father's Love Begotten

C. Michael Hawn, "History of Hymns: 'Of Father's Love Begotten,'" *Discipleship Ministries of The United Methodist Church* (website), 24 June 2013; available at https://www.umcdiscipleship.org /resources/history-of-hymns-of-the-fathers-love-begotten; accessed 13 December 2021.

Mormon Tabernacle Choir, *Hallelujah!* (music CD; 2016).

"Of the Father's Love Begotten," John Mason Neale, trans., *Trinity Psalter Hymnal* (Willow Grove, PA: 2018), no. 268.

"Aurelius Clemens Prudentius," in *A Dictionary of Hymnology: Setting Forth the Origin and History of Christian Hymns of All Ages and Nations,* Volume 2, edited by John Julian (New York: Dover Publications, 1907), 914–15.

Lo, How a Rose E'er Blooming

Robert D. Hawkins, *Prelude and Fugue on the Life of Harriet Reynolds Krauth Spaeth 1845–1925: Shaping American Lutheran Church Music* (Minneapolis, MN: Lutheran University Press, 2013).

C. Michael Hawn, "History of Hymns: Hymn presents Savior as 'Rose e'er blooming,'" *Discipleship Ministries of The United Methodist Church* (website), 30 May 2013; available at https://www.umcdiscipleship .org/resources/history-of-hymns-hymn-presents-savior-as-rose-eer -blooming; accessed 10 December 2021.

Patrick M. Liebergan, ed., "Lo, How a Rose E're Blooming," in *Singer's Library of Song: A Vocal Anthology of Masterworks and Folk Songs from the Medieval Era through the Twentieth Century* (Los Angeles: Alfred Publishing, 2005), 122–26.

"Lo, How a Rose E're Blooming," *United Methodist Hymnal*, 216.

Mormon Tabernacle Choir, *Merry Christmas with the Mormon Tabernacle Choir* (music CD; 2015).

Hark! The Herald Angels Sing

A Collection of Hymns for Use of the People Called Methodists, John Wesley, ed. (London, 1779).

Andrew Gant, *Carols of Christmas*, 106–17.

C. Michael Hawn, "History of Hymns: 'Hark! The Herald Angels Sing,'" *Discipleship Ministries of The United Methodist Church* (website), 11 December 2014; available at https://www.umcdiscipleship.org /resources/history-of-hymns-hark-the-herald-angels-sing; accessed 13 December 2021.

Mark Lawson-Jones, *Why Was the Partridge in the Pear Tree?* 76–81.

The Tabernacle Choir at Temple Square, *Angels among Us* (music CD; 2019).

Charles Wesley, "Hark! The Herald Angels Sing," *United Methodist Hymnal*, 240.

Away in a Manger

"Away in a Manger," *United Methodist Hymnal*, 217.

Chris Fenner, "Away in a Manger," *Hymnology Archive* (website), 5 December 2018; available at https://www.hymnologyarchive.com /away-in-a-manger; accessed 13 December 2021.

Andrew Gant, *Carols of Christmas*, 120–26.

C. Michael Hawn, "History of Hymns: 'Away in a Manger,'" *Discipleship Ministries of The United Methodist Church* (website), 7 June 2013; available at https://www.umcdiscipleship.org/resources/history-of -hymns-away-in-a-manger; accessed 13 December 2021.

Mormon Tabernacle Choir, *Sing, Choirs of Angels!* (music CD; 2004).

Angels from the Realms of Glory

Andrew Gant, *Carols of Christmas,* 96–104.

C. Michael Hawn, "History of Hymns: 'Angels from the Realms of Glory,'" *Discipleship Ministries of The United Methodist Church* (website), June 19, 2013; available at https://www.umcdiscipleship.org /resources/history-of-hymns-angels-from-the-realms-of-glory-1; ac- cessed 13 December 2021.

James Montgomery, *The Wanderer of Switzerland, and Other Poems* (Boston: J. Belcher, 1812).

Mormon Tabernacle Choir, *Ring Christmas Bells* (music CD; 2009).

Robert T. Williamson, "The Religious Thought of James Montgomery"

(PhD thesis), University of Edinburgh, 1950; available at https://era
.ed.ac.uk/bitstream/handle/1842/10190/0074214c.pdf; accessed 13
December 2021.

Masters in This Hall

Doug Anderson, "Masters in This Hall," *Hymns and Carols of Christmas*
(website); available at https://www.hymnsandcarolsofchristmas
.com/Hymns_and_Carols/masters_in_this_hall-1.htm; accessed 13
December 2021.

*A Christmas Garland: Carols and Poems from the Fifteenth Century to the
Present Time*, A. H. Bullen, ed. (London: John C. Nimmo, 1885),
80–83.

Mormon Tabernacle Choir, *A Mormon Tabernacle Choir Christmas* (music
CD; 2000).

O du Fröhliche (O You Joyful)

Maria Berg, "O you joyful," *Deutsche Welle* (website), 22 December 2013;
available at https://www.dw.com/en/o-you-joyful/a-17313920; accessed 13 December 2021.

"*O du Fröhliche: A German Christmas Carol in German and English*," *The
German Way & More* (website); available at https://www.german-way
.com/history-and-culture/german-language/german-christmas-carols
/o-du-frohliche/; accessed 13 December 2021.

"*O du fröhliche*," *Hymnary* (website); available at https://hymnary.org/text
/o_du_froeliche_o_du_selige_weihnachtszei; accessed 13 December
2021.

"*O du Fröhliche! O du Selige*," in *New Oxford Book of Carols*, 594–96.

Wiener Sängerknaben / Vienna Boys' Choir, *Sacred Choral Music* (music
CD; 2019).

In the Bleak Midwinter

"Bleak Midwinter named best carol," *BBC News* (website), 27 November
2008; available at http://news.bbc.co.uk/2/hi/entertainment/arts
_and_culture/7752029.stm; accessed 13 December 2021.

Kathleen Jones, *Learning Not to Be First: The Life of Christina Rossetti* (New York: St. Martin's, 1992).

Mark Lawson-Jones, *Why Was the Partridge in the Pear Tree?* 122–28.

Mormon Tabernacle Choir, *The Most Wonderful Time of the Year* (music CD; 2016).

Karen Swallow Prior, "The Remarkable Woman Behind 'In the Bleak Midwinter,'" *The Gospel Coalition* (website), 16 December 2015; available at https://www.thegospelcoalition.org/article/the-remarkable-woman-behind-in-the-bleak-midwinter/; accessed 13 December 2021.

Christina Rossetti, "A Christmas Hymn," *Scribner's Monthly,* vol. 1, no. 3 (1 January 1872): 278.

———. "In the Bleak Midwinter," *United Methodist Hymnal,* 221.

The First Noel

Ace Collins, *Stories behind the Best-Loved Songs of Christmas* (Grand Rapids, MI: Zondervan, 2001), 36–42.

"The First Noel," in *New Oxford Book of Carols,* 478–83.

C. Michael Hawn, "History of Hymns: 'The First Noel,'" *Discipleship Ministries of The United Methodist Church* (website), 31 December 2020; available at https://www.umcdiscipleship.org/articles/history-of-hymns-the-first-noel; accessed 13 December 2021.

Mormon Tabernacle Choir, *The Wonder of Christmas* (music CD; 2006).

Infant Holy, Infant Lowly

C. Michael Hawn, "History of Hymns: 'Infant Holy, Infant Lowly,'" *Discipleship Ministries of the United Methodist Church* (website), 17 December 2015; available at https://www.umcdiscipleship.org/resources/history-of-hymns-infant-holy-infant-lowly-1; accessed 13 December 2021.

"Infant Holy, Infant Lowly," *Hymnary* (website); available at https://hymnary.org/text/infant_holy_infant_lowly; accessed 13 December 2021.

Edith M. G. Reed, trans., "Infant Holy, Infant Lowly," *United Methodist Hymnal,* 229.

The Tabernacle Choir at Temple Square, *Christmas Best* (music CD; 2021).

Nancy Byrd Turner, "Stars Were Gleaming," in *Hymns for Primary Worship* (Philadelphia: Westminster Press, 1946).

Stille Nacht (Silent Night)

Mark Lawson-Jones, *Why Was the Partridge in the Pear Tree?* 102–7.

Joseph Mohr, "Silent Night, Holy Night," *United Methodist Hymnal,* 239.

———. "*Stille Nacht, heilige Nacht,*" *Gesangbuch* (Frankfurt am Main: Kirche Jesu Christi der Heiligen der Letzten Tage, 1996), no. 134.

Edward W. Schmidt, "'Silent Night' turns 200 this year: Is it the greatest Christmas song ever?" *American Jesuit Review* (website), 24 December 2018; available at https://www.americamagazine.org/arts-culture /2018/12/06/silent-night-turns-200-year-it-greatest-christmas -song-ever; accessed 13 December 2021.

Stille Nacht Museum (website), Hallein, Austria; available at https:// stillenacht.com; accessed 13 December 2021.

The Tabernacle Choir at Temple Square, *Christmas Best* (music CD; 2021).

Stanley Weintraub, *Silent Night: The Story of the World War I Christmas Truce* (New York: Free Press, 2001).

About the Author

Michael D. Young is a graduate of Brigham Young University and Western Governors University with degrees in German teaching, music, educational leadership, and instructional design. Though he grew up traveling the world with his military father, he now lives in Utah with his wife, Jen, and their three children, where he teaches in a German dual-language immersion program. He enjoys acting in community theater, playing and writing music, and spending time with his family. He played for several years with the handbell choir Bells on Temple Square and is now a member of The Tabernacle Choir at Temple Square.

He is the author of the novels in the Canticle Kingdom series, the Last Archangel series, the Chess Quest series, and the Penultimate Dawn series, as well as several nonfiction works, including *The Song of the Righteous, As*

Saints We Sing, and *The Song of the Saints*. He has also had work featured in various online and print magazines such as *Bards and Sages Quarterly*, *Mindflights*, *Meridian*, *Nugent Magazine*, *The New Era*, *Keeping Tab*, *Allegory*, *Liahona*, and *Ensign*. He has won honorable mention three times in the Writers of the Future contest.

He runs several podcasts, including *Chapter and Verse*, *The Carols of Christmas*, and *Songs for All Seasons*. Learn more at www.authormichaelyoung.com.